At Teita's Table

My grandchildren's favorite traditional Lebanese recipes made simple

Recipes by Nadia Ghubril Abuhamad
Edited and compiled by Sana Abuhamad Pratt

*To all my grandchildren,
hoping that they enjoy the recipes
of the cuisine of our heritage.*

Table of Contents

صحتين

Introduction

When my brothers and I were growing up, our mom cooked for us every day without fail. I'm not sure we fully appreciated how lucky we were to sit together as a family and bond over the day's events while we ate the very finest Lebanese cuisine. As her only daughter, my appreciation for her self-taught talents as a cook and her ability to make a familiar Lebanese dish something truly special has only grown over the years.

I think all of our children assume that Teita's brilliance (Teita means grandmother in Arabic) in the kitchen was simply something passed down from her mother via the usual oral traditions that are common in Lebanon. But this isn't true. She was one of five daughters and didn't usually work with her mother in the kitchen. My brothers and I (and now our families) are always entertained by her story of how, early in her marriage, Jiddo (my father) came home with dinner guests and an enormous fish - head, eyes, tail and scales - for her to cook! She was completely lost, and perhaps this moment, with a fish laying on the counter staring up at her, was the beginning of her culinary journey: a journey of trial and error, intuition, creativity, precision, tenacity, and intellect.

Through this cookbook, her journey is carried on for all of us. It isn't simply that the food is wonderfully good (it always is!), but her meals are about family time around the table, connections, love, and the idea that we will be with and for each other throughout our lives. We can look beyond today and realize that our children and grandchildren will share time around the table laughing and building permanent bonds with each other.

I have loved joining in on this journey by translating Teita's "oral tradition" into recipes. In many cases I have myself learnt how to prepare these meals truly well for the first time, though I have been watching Teita cook since I was a little girl. Over and over again we cooked the dishes and tested the recipes. We "Skyped", "Facetimed", talked (even hollered a bit at times!), took pictures (and more pictures), tasted, shopped, and debated every detail until we were sure we had it just right. By transforming the visuals and approximations of the oral tradition (i.e. add a bit of cinnamon, or just add a small amount of yogurt) into actual measurements, the dishes can now be reproduced consistently and with confidence.

What follows is a collection of our family favorites. Though some recipes require some labor, the majority can be whipped up in minimal time and the result is a healthy, delicious Lebanese meal.

Our shared goal is to inspire the Lebanese chef in you.

Sana

صحتين

Cookbook Guide

Each recipe is written to help you avoid the common mistakes I made along the way (and I made more than a few!) and to learn new food preparation techniques. Be sure to first read "The Lebanese Kitchen" section (pages 13-15), which includes menu suggestions, and a list of essential and frequently used ingredients and equipment (some not likely found in your kitchen).

The recipe's title is given in phonetic Arabic, in Arabic, and the translation in English. Main ingredients of the recipe are shown in the row of pictures under the title of the dish – a quick scan will tell you what you need before you start cooking. The number of Lebanese chef hats (or toques) indicates the difficulty of a recipe, with one toque ♨ being easy, two toques ♨♨ meaning a bit complex, and three toques ♨♨♨ indicating complex.

Before tackling a recipe, read the directions thoroughly. Note that because including cook times alone doesn't guarantee the result (no two ovens or pans are alike), I've also included descriptions of what to look for so you know when dish is ready to serve. Along with each recipe I've made suggestions for what might best accompany a dish, as well as hints and tips on buying, storing, or preparing the ingredients.

Finally, the word "Sahtain" is written in Arabic at bottom of each left-hand page. It means "double health" and this is what we hope you'll always have as you enjoy cooking and sharing new meals with friends and family.

صحتين

The Lebanese Kitchen

The Lebanese kitchen is founded on simple ingredients of excellent quality. Most of what you need is available at the neighborhood supermarket, or at international food markets. Choose and cook what looks fresh and in season.

As you will see, the ingredient pictures at the top of each recipe do not include the basic spices in the recipe. That is because it is expected that the Lebanese kitchen will have at least these spices on the spice rack: salt (1), whole black pepper (2), ground black pepper (3), cinnamon (4), nutmeg (5), coriander (6), chili flakes (7) (or cayenne pepper), cardamom pods (8), and bay leaves (9).

You will also need to stock and have on hand a few other important ingredients, namely, onions, garlic, lemons, and olive oil. Because olive oil is drizzled on top of food, e.g. hommos, baba ghanouj, and therefore eaten raw, it's preferable that you buy extra virgin olive oil or whatever tastes good to you.

You'll find that we use parsley (10) in different dishes, tabbouleh, kafta, salads, etc. So, it's a good idea to have some picked, and washed, and ready to go. The best way to store parsley is to spread the washed and dried parsley on a clean kitchen towel (or paper towels) and roll the towel and parsley together. Place the towel in a plastic bag and put in the vegetable drawer in the fridge. It should keep for 2-3 days.

Cilantro (11) is a common ingredient used in stews. Since it is usually cooked, you can store washed, chopped cilantro in a ziplock bag in the freezer. Just add it while still frozen to the cooking pot.

Burghul (12) is a Lebanese ingredient used in many recipes, fresh and cooked. It is made from wheat groats that are picked, boiled until the kernel breaks open, drained and put to dry. The dried wheat is taken to a mill to grind into coarse, medium, and fine burghul, each for a different use. The finest ground, #1, for tabbouleh and kibbeh, #2 medium ground or #3 coarsest ground for burghul bi banadoora, #3 (not used in the recipes in this book) can also be used in dishes that require a longer cooking time.

Zaa'tar , a special combination of herbs and spices, is made from the flower of the Middle Eastern wild thyme (Thymus capitatus). After drying, the flowers are ground to a powder, and mixed with salt and sumac. For every pound of zaa'tar flowers, a 1/2 pound of sumac and a 1/4 cup kosher salt is added. Finally, a 1/2 pound toasted sesame seeds is mixed in. Zaa'tar from other Middle Eastern countries might include one or more other spice such as cumin, fennel, caraway, oregano, garlic powder, coriander, anise.

Tahini , a Middle Eastern sesame paste, made from ground hulled toasted sesame seeds, is now very popular and can be found as a healthy ingredient in every day recipes from salad dressings to granola.

Pomegranate molasses  is a Middle Eastern syrup that is sweet and tart. It's intense, so a little goes a long way. It's made by boiling down pomegranate juice. It can be used in the bamyeh bi zeit (okra sauté), over roasted vegetables and in meat dishes, such as lahmeh bi ajine. It is also tasty over desserts, ice cream, roasted fruits, etc.

Rose water and orange blossom water  are fragrant, floral flavors added to Mediterranean and Middle Eastern desserts. They are made from high quality rose or orange blossom petals that are steamed and the condensate is collected. For a more intense flavor and aroma, add either or both after completing the cooking, for example after the sugar syrup has come to the right consistency and the heat is turned off. If baked, the essence mellows out and the aroma is more subtle.

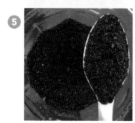

Sumac (not poison sumac - though related) is a Mediterranean wild berry, ground and used to add sour flavor when lemons are not available, or when tartness is needed without additional acid or liquid (as in zaa'tar and fattoush). For a pop of deep red color, sprinkle the sumac on dips like hommos, and baba ghanouj.

A few pieces of special equipment are needed. The recipes frequently require crushing the garlic with the salt. For this, a small wooden mortar and pestle is used **6** .

The result is actually creamed garlic **7** . Creaming the garlic is important because the garlic, whether cooked or raw, is meant to dissolve in the dish, and should not be crunched on when the meal is eaten.

For making Lebanese coffee, you will need an ibrik **8** , a special pot with a spout. It is usually made of thin metals that conduct heat quickly to allow the water to boil fast. The handle is long, so that the end of the handle stays cool for you to move the ibrik on and off the heat as you make the coffee.

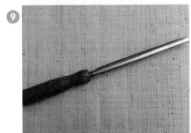

To make Stuffed Cousa you will need a coussa or zucchini corer **9** . It has a handle with a sharp curved blade so that you can insert and twist the blade to remove the seeds and cores from coussa (or any other fruit or vegetable).

صحتين

Suggested Menus

As a general rule, every Lebanese table at every meal will have pita bread, as well as a plate with fresh vegetables even if a salad is served. Also included on the table is a small plate of olives to be eaten along and after the meal. Dessert is usually seasonal fruits.

When designing menus, ingredient variety is the deciding factor. So, if you have tabbouleh listed on the menu, usually, the other items on the menu should not contain a lot of parsley (for example, kafta), and should not contain burghul (for example kibbeh). The Lebanese cooked what was seasonally available, and so the combinations of ingredients were made by nature. Tabbouleh was a spring and summer dish and usually eaten outside on the porch or balcony to enjoy the weather. Dried legumes and other meals based on grains e.g. mjadra, were big in winter since it was hard to get fresh vegetables. We are pleasantly spoiled now with all fruits and vegetables available year round, whether fresh or frozen.

The following are suggested menus. If they seem daunting, don't worry – add or subtract whatever you like. Just remember, planning is key. In order to make a feast, you need a party trick – working ahead. Some dishes you can refrigerate (for a day or two) or freeze (up to a two weeks) after partially baking. For example kibbeh, you can half-bake it (bake for 15 minutes instead of 30 minutes) and freeze it on Monday, then thaw and complete the baking for a Saturday night dinner party. For salads e.g. tabbouleh, you can prepare the different components ahead of time, and keep them covered but unmixed in the bowl in the fridge. The next day, before serving, you add the dressing and mix. Or you can make large batches of stew meat, which can then be portioned out and frozen for different meals. Pull out a meal portion from the freezer in the morning to thaw, and use it after work in one of the stew recipes for a quick, healthy 30-minute dinner – remarkably convenient!

Breakfast / Brunch menus:

Knaffeh bi Jibin (p.119), seasonal fruits
Mana'eesh (p.103), cheese, labneh, cut tomatoes and cucumbers

Lunch / Dinner menus:

Summer menus:

Tabbouleh (p.31), Hommos (p.35), Teita's Rice (p.45), Yakhnet Loubyeh (p.75) or Yakhnet Bamyeh (p.71)

Tabbouleh (p.31), Baba Ghanouj (p.37), Flayfleh Mihshiyeh maa' Banadoora (p.85)

Autumn menus:

Fattoush (p.29), Hommos (p.35), Coussa Mihshi wa Warak Aareesh (p.97)

Tabbouleh (p.31), Baba Ghanouj (p.37), Djaj bi Toom (p.57), Fatayer bi Sabanekh (p.107)

Winter dishes:

Cabbage Salata (p.27), Burghul bi Banadoora (p.43), Mjadra (p.83), Lifit (p.125)

Salata (p.27), Hommos (p.35), Teita's Rice (p.45), Yakhnet Fassoulia (p.79)

Spring:

Salata (p.27), Teita's Rice (p.45), Yakhnet Bazella (p.73), Fatayer bi Sabanekh (p.107)

Fattoosh (p.29), Loubyeh bi Zeit (p.39), Kafta bil Sayniyeh (p.61)

And now, put on your Lebanese chef hat and let's get started!

Drinks

1
An Ibrik is usually made of thin metals (copper or stainless steel) that conduct heat quickly to allow the water to boil fast. The handle is long, so that the end of the handle stays cool for you to move the ibrik on and off the heat.

Kahwah قهوة

Lebanese Coffee

Lebanese coffee is between espresso and Turkish coffee. It is strong and flavorful, and good for sipping while visiting with friends. You can purchase Lebanese coffee grounds with or without cardamom at international and Middle Eastern markets. The dark roasted, finely ground coffee is vacuum packed in 200-gram and 500-gram bags. Ater opening, reseal well and store in the freezer to retain freshness. Use an ibrik to brew the coffee ❶.

Total time: 5-7 minutes   Serves 2

1 cup water

1 teaspoon sugar (optional)

3 tablespoons Lebanese coffee grounds

1. Pour water in the ibrik, but do not fill to the top. Use bigger ibrik if necessary. Bring water to boil on medium heat. Add sugar and bring back to boil.

2. Remove from heat. Gently add the coffee with stirring. Be careful when adding the coffee so that it doesn't foam and overflow.

3. Put back on low heat, and allow to foam, removing from the heat just prior to overflowing. Foam, stir and return to heat a couple more times. When you see a small clearing in the foam, it's done.

4. Serve in espresso cups.

Notes

Coffee is served anytime guests arrive. Often, on the same tray as the coffee will be a glass of water with added orange blossom water (1 cup water with a 1/2 tsp of orange blossom water). It is likely that the first few times (or even when you become an expert coffee maker) the coffee will overflow. No worries. It makes a bit of a mess, but, as the saying goes in Lebanon, "Kab el ahweh kheir" or "spilled coffee is a blessing".

A distilled alcohol drink made from grapes with anise seed flavor added. It is a colorless liquid that turns white when you add water. Served as an aperitif or throughout the meal.

In whatever glass you are using, the ratio of arak to water is 1:3. In a glass, add the arak, then add the water, and ice if desired. Enjoy with Mezze.

Mezze مزه

Small plates of goodies to nibble on while enjoying a drink.

There are multiple levels of mezze, but each one should include at least the basics: Bzourat (a mixture of roasted and salted nuts and seeds) **1**, cut fresh vegetables, Lebanese olives or zeitoon (black or green olives cured in brine and herbs then preserved in olive oil) **2**, cheese, or labneh (plain yogurt, strained overnight, served with salt and olive oil), and pickled vegetables.

A bit fancier mezze would include spinach triangles (page 107), kibbeh balls (page 69), hommos (page 35), and baba ghanouj (page 37). The highest echelons of mezze would include lahmeh bi ajin (page 111), raw kibbeh, and organ meat such as liver, brains, kidneys prepared in special ways. And this is all before the main meal is served!

1 بزورات
Bzourat

2 زيتون
Zeitoon

Salads

1

Add the lemon
juice to the garlic
and mix before
pouring onto
veggies.

Salata سَلَطة

Lebanese Salad

Active time: 10 minutes

VG Serves 4

Basic dressing:

**2 cloves garlic, peeled, crushed with 1
teaspoon salt**

1/3 cup fresh lemon juice

2 tablespoons olive oil

Add the lemon juice to the garlic and mix well.
Pour garlic/lemon mixture over 4 cups fresh
cut vegetables, your choice: lettuce, tomatoes,
cucumber, peppers, green or sweet onions. Add
olive oil. Mix well. Serve immediately.

The same dressing is used for:

1. **Sliced cabbage salad:** pour dressing over 4
   cups sliced cabbage. For color, you can add
   a diced tomato, or a diced, cooked beet.
   Sprinkle hot chili flakes on top for extra spice.

2. **Potato salad:** pour dressing over 4 cups of
   diced, boiled, peeled potatoes. Add 1/2 cup
   green onions and 1/2 cup chopped parsley.

3. **Legumes:** Mix dressing into 1.5 cups cooked
   legumes, e.g. canned foulle (small fava bean),
   or cooked, canned chickpeas. Add 1/2 cup
   chopped parsley.

Eat with

Foulle or chickpeas with additional olive oil,
fresh pita bread, and green onions.

Fattoush, ready to serve.

1

Sumac

Middle Eastern wild berries, ground and used to add sour flavor when lemons are not available, or when tartness is needed without additional acid or liquid.

صحتين

Fattoush فتوش

Large Salad with Pita Bread

The sumac is optional but really adds a lot to the taste.

Active time: 30 minutes

 VG Serves 6

1/2 loaf of pita bread

3 cloves garlic

1 tablespoon salt

1/2 cup lemon juice

1 cup sliced cucumber

1 tomato cut into bite size cubes

1 cup sliced lettuce

1/2 cup chopped green onions, white and green parts (or any kind of onion)

1 cup chopped parsley

1/2 cup chopped mint

1/4 cup olive oil

1 tablespoon sumac (optional) ❶

1. Crush garlic with salt. Add lemon juice and mix. Put the mixture in a big bowl.

2. Add all vegetables to the bowl.

3. Just before serving, toast the bread, break into bite size pieces, and add to the vegetables. If using, sprinkle the sumac on top of the bread.

4. Add oil, mix well and serve immediately while the bread is still crunchy.

1 Picked parsley.

2 Desired chop for parsley/mint combination.

Tabbouleh تبوله
Special Traditional Lebanese Salad

Active time: 30 minutes   Parsley prep: 2.5 hours

  Serves 4

Advance planning:

Pick the parsley ❶ and place picked parsley and mint mix in a large bowl. Cover with water and let sit for a few minutes to allow sand and sediment to sink to the bottom of the bowl. Remove parsley and mint from the water and place in colander. Pour out water remaining in the bowl, noting sediment in the bottom. Repeat process until no sediment is visible in the bottom of the bowl. Let parsley strain and dry in colander for a couple hours.

3 tablespoons brown burghul ground #1

3 tablespoons fresh lemon juice

1/2 cup onion, yellow, green, red or a combination, finely chopped

1/2 teaspoon salt

1/4 teaspoon allspice, pepper, or both

1/2 pound tomatoes, chopped

2 cups packed parsley, picked, washed

1/2 cup fresh spearmint leaves, picked, washed

3 Tablespoons olive oil

1. Put burghul in a bowl, add lemon juice and let sit to soak.
2. Add onions to burghul in bowl. Add salt, allspice and pepper and mix into onions. Add tomatoes.
3. Finely chop parsley/mint combination (see desired chop in ❷) and add to the bowl.
4. Add olive oil and mix well.

Note

Do the prep work ahead of time and keep bowl covered in the fridge for up to 8 hours. Just before serving, add oil and mix well.

Eat with

Fresh romaine lettuce and/or fresh soft cabbage leaves from the heart of the cabbage for scooping up the tabbouleh.

Side Dishes

1 After soaking overnight, chickpeas will double in size.

2 Cooked chickpeas get mushy when pressed down with a spoon.

صحتين

Hommos   حمص

There are lots of variations on hommos out there, but this is the traditional Lebanese recipe.

Overnight soak   Active time: 30 minutes   Cook time: 2 hours   VG   Serves 4

Advance planning:
The chickpeas need to be soaked overnight.

1 cup dried chick peas
2 teaspoons baking soda, divided
1 bay leaf
3 tablespoon lemon juice
2 cloves peeled garlic, crushed with 1 tsp salt
3 tablespoon tahini

1. Put chickpeas in a large bowl and mix with 1 teaspoon baking soda. Cover with water 2 inches above level of chickpeas. Soak overnight. Chickpeas will double in size ❶.

2. Next day, drain the chickpeas and wash with water. Place in a large pot, add the other teaspoon baking soda, the bay leaf, and cold water to cover by 2 inches. Bring to a boil and let simmer on low, partially covered, for 2 hours.

Note

If you have a pressure cooker, you can cook the chickpeas directly without soaking. Do not add the baking soda.

3. When the chickpeas are soft and mushy ❷, take off the heat. Drain and save about 1 cup of cooking liquid.

4. While still hot, put chickpeas in food processor, add garlic and lemon, and puree until smooth.

5. Add the tahini and puree some more adding cooking liquid by teaspoonfuls if the mixture is dry.

6. You can serve now, but keep in mind that flavors deepen and improve overnight in fridge.

7. If you refrigerate it, next day, remove from fridge and let sit at room temperature to soften. Stir and adjust seasoning, if necessary.

Eat with

A drizzle of olive oil, green onions, and pita bread.

1 Eggplant on burner.

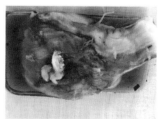

2 Peeled roasted eggplant.

Baba Ghanouj بابا غنوج

Good as a side dish or a dip with cut vegetables.

Active time: 30 min

VG Serves 4

1 pound Italian eggplant
2 cloves garlic, crushed with 1 teaspoon salt
1/3 cup fresh lemon juice
2 tablespoon tahini

1. Cook the eggplant whole (with green stem). You can char it by placing it directly on the stovetop burner ❶. If broiling in the oven, make several incisions in the eggplant with a sharp knife and place it in a pan under the oven broiler. Turn the eggplant as it chars and softens. Watch your fingers. It's fine if it leaks juice.

2. When cooked through and all parts of the eggplant are soft, remove from heat, place in a dish and let cool for a few minutes before peeling. You can also rinse the cooked eggplant in cold water to help the peeling process. While still warm, remove the skin and cut the green stem off the eggplant ❷.

3. Put the peeled eggplant in the processor. Add the lemon juice to the crushed garlic and mix well. Add lemon/garlic mix to the eggplant in processor. Add the tahini and process until the ingredients are thoroughly mixed and the baba ghanouj is creamy.

Eat with

Pita bread, olive oil, green onions and radishes.

Note

Keeps well in the fridge, well covered. Let come to room temperature to soften before serving.

1
Green
beans cut
into 2 inch
pieces.

Loubyeh bi Zeit لوبيه بزيت

Green Bean Sauté

Active time: 15 minutes   Cooking time 45 minutes   VG Serves 4

1 pound green beans (fresh or frozen, cut)

1 onion, chopped

2 tablespoons olive oil

6 garlic cloves, whole

2 tomatoes, diced (about 1 cup)

1 bunch fresh cilantro, picked, washed, and chopped

1 teaspoon salt

1. Heat olive oil in medium size saucepan and sauté the onion and garlic until soft.

2. Add the green beans and sauté for a few minutes, turning over so that the beans get coated with oil, about 5 minutes.

3. Add the tomatoes, cilantro, and 1 teaspoon salt. Mix well.

4. Cover and cook on low for 30 minutes, or until the beans are soft and the tomato juice is absorbed.

Eat with

Pita bread, green onions, green peppers.

Note

Buying and preparing fresh green beans: Choose green beans that are crisp enough to snap in half. Avoid yellow, brown or bruised beans. Beans can be stored in the vegetable drawer for a few days. Before using, trim ends of green beans and any strings that come off while clipping the ends. Snap the bean in about 2-inch pieces . Rinse in colander and allow to drain.

صحتين

Bamyeh bi Zeit باميه بزيت
Okra Sauté with Tomatoes

Active time: 15 minutes   **Cooking time: 45 minutes**   VG **Serves 4**

1 pound okra (frozen whole or cut)
1 onion, chopped
6 garlic cloves, peeled, whole
2 tomatoes, diced (about 1 cup)
1 bunch fresh cilantro, picked, washed, and chopped
1 teaspoon salt
1 tablespoon pomegranate molasses (optional)

1. In a frying pan, sauté the onion and garlic with 2 tablespoons oil until soft.

2. Add okra and sauté for a few minutes, without stirring.

3. Add the tomatoes and the cilantro. Sprinkle 1 teaspoon salt over the mixture in pan.

4. Cover and cook on low for 30 minutes, or until the okra is soft and the juice from the tomatoes is absorbed.

5. If using, drizzle the pomegranate molasses on top of the okra and mix in gently.

Eat with
Pita bread, green onions.

Pomegranate molasses is a Middle Eastern syrup that is sweet and tart. It's made by boiling down pomegranate juice. It can be used in the okra sauté, over roasted vegetables and in meat dishes, such as lahme bi ajine. It can also be tasty over desserts, ice cream, roasted fruits, etc. It's intense, similar to balsamic vinegar, so a little goes a long way.

Note
Try not to disturb the okra too much while cooking so it doesn't become slimy.

1 Slice onions.

2 Sauté onions.

Burghul bi Banadoora برغل بي بندورة

Burghul with Tomato and Cabbage

Active time: 15 minutes   **Cooking time: 45 minutes**   Serves 4

1 onion, sliced ❶

1 cup diced tomato

3 cups shredded cabbage (green or white)

1/2 cup burghul medium #2

Note

For a gluten free version, substitute quinoa for the burghul.

Sauté onion in 2 tablespoons of oil until soft ❷. Add tomatoes and cabbage ❸. Sprinkle 1/2 teaspoon salt over cabbage. Cover and allow cabbage to wilt on low heat until soft and juices are released, stirring occasionally, about 15 minutes. Add the burghul (or quinoa) ❹, stir to distribute evenly. Cover and cook on low heat until the burghul is soft and no longer crunchy, stirring occasionally, about 30 minutes.

❸ Sliced cabbage & chopped tomatoes are added.

❹ Burghul or quinoa added.

Roz Teita رز تيتا

Teita's Rice

Comfort food at its best! Traditionally, served with a sprinkle of ground cinnamon on top.

Active time: 10 minutes   Cooking time: 30 minutes

 Serves 4

1 cup white rice, any kind, long grain or short grain

1 tablespoon butter, salted or unsalted

1/3 cup dried vermicelli, cracked

1/2 teaspoon salt

1 cup boiling water or hot chicken broth

1. Wash rice. Place in medium bowl, cover with cold water, swirl gently with your hand a few times, then drain by tilting the bowl gently to once side, allowing the cloudy water to pour out while catching falling rice grains with your other hand.

2. In a pan, melt butter, add vermicelli and stir. Watch carefully since it burns easily.

3. When the noodles are gold in color, add the drained rice and 1 teaspoon salt. Mix with the fried noodles.

4. Add 1 cup boiling water. Bring back to boil and let boil 5 minutes. Stir rice once to make sure it is not stuck to the bottom of the pan.

5. Reduce heat, cover and simmer on low for 20 minutes.

Note

The rice can be included as a side for many vegetable stews, e.g. green bean stew, okra stew, ablama batinjan, but also as a side for dishes that can be eaten with yogurt, e.g. kafta, kibbeh, etc. In Lebanon, rice with plain yogurt is a very typical meal for small children that do not want to eat the vegetable stew.

صحتين

Na'rat Coussa نقرات كوسا
Coussa Cores with Eggs

Active time: 15 minutes   **Total time: 30 minutes**   **Serves 2**

This is a good and delicious use of the coussa squash cores from **Coussa Mihshi** and any coussa that was poked through with the corer and could not be stuffed. In fact, you don't have to wait until you have cores, you can make it anytime with any kind of squash, by cutting the whole squash into small cubes so that it cooks quickly. Good for breakfast, brunch, or a light meal.

About 1/2 cup coussa squash cores (from 4 coussa – if you have coussa that was poked during coring, you can chop it into ¼ inch cubes and use it here)

1/2 cup chopped onion

2 tablespoons olive oil, divided

1/2 teaspoon each salt, pepper, cinnamon

2 eggs

1. In a saucepan, heat 1 tablespoon olive oil and add onions. Sauté until soft and translucent.

2. Add the coussa cores and/or chopped coussa squash and cook on low heat until soft and cooked through. Sprinkle with salt, pepper and cinnamon.

3. Make an opening in the center of the pan for the eggs by pushing the cooked coussa/onion combination to the edges of the pan. Pour 1 tablespoon olive oil into the cleared center and crack two eggs into the oil. You can leave the eggs sunnyside up, or mix it into the coussa. Cook until the eggs are done.

Eat with
Pita bread, fresh green peppers, fresh green onions.

1 Cooked lentils.

2 Slice onions.

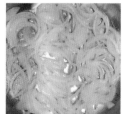
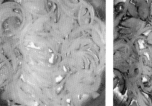

3 Caramelize onions in skillet over medium heat until dark brown.

صحتين

Mdardra مدردة

Lentils with Caramelized Onions

Lentils, rice, and caramelized onions never tasted so good.

Active & cooking time: 1 hour   VG Serves 4

1 cup rice
1/2 cup large green lentils, picked from any
**   stones, and rinsed with water**
1 cup sliced onions
1 teaspoon salt
1 tablespoon butter

1. Wash rice. Place in a medium bowl, cover with cold water, swirl gently with your hand a few times, then drain by tilting the bowl gently to one side, allowing the cloudy water to pour out while catching falling rice grains with your other hand. Set aside.

2. Place rinsed lentils in a medium saucepan, add 2 cups water. Boil until the lentils are cooked but have not lost their structure, about 30 minutes ❶. Drain the lentils and reserve the lentil water for cooking the rice in the next step.

3. In the same saucepan, sauté the onions until light brown. Add the rice and sauté for one minute, stirring to mix with the onions. Add the lentil water, about 11/2 cups, then add the cooked lentils. Add 1 teaspoon salt. Bring to boil, then simmer on low until the rice is cooked and all liquid is absorbed, about 30 minutes. Gently stir in the butter.

4. Decorate with caramelized onions.

Caramelized onions

1 large onion, sliced
Dash of salt
Vegetable oil

1. Using a stainless steel or cast iron skillet large enough to spead the onions into one layer, place skillet over medium heat. Add oil, enough to cover the bottom of the skillet. Add the sliced onions and stir gently. Sprinkle some salt over the onions and let cook, stirring every few minutes.

2. Continue cooking and stirring until the onions are dark brown and caramelized. (Various stages of caramelization shown in ❸). Keep watch so they don't burn. It could take from 20 to 50 minutes, depending on the pan and the amount of onions.

Eat with

Plain yogurt, olives, radishes, green onions, tomatoes, fresh mint, pickled turnips (lift), pickled cucumbers.

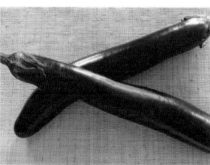

You can use Japanese eggplant instead of the Italian eggplant in this recipe. Just slice it into 1-inch round slices, no need to peel since the skin is thin, and no need to salt and drain since it's sweet. Fry the eggplant slices until soft and lightly browned, then use in step 4.

Mnazleh منزله

Eggplant, Chickpeas, and Tomato Sauté

Good vegan recipe, satisfying with a lot of flavor.

Active time: 30 minutes   Cooking time: 30 minutes

 VG Serves 4

Advance planning:
Chickpeas need to be soaked overnight.

1 pound Italian eggplant

1 1/2 cups diced tomatoes

1/2 cup chickpeas, soaked overnight

2 cups onions, thinly sliced

1/2 cup vegetable oil, divided

1. **Chickpeas:** Wash and drain the chickpeas and spread on a paper towel to dry. Roll with a rolling pin to peel and split. Remove peels. Put the split peas in a pan with water. Boil until cooked but not mushy, about 15 minutes. Drain and put aside.

2. **Eggplant:** Peel the eggplant and cut into 1 inch cubes. Sprinkle with 1/2 teaspoon salt and let sit for 10 minutes to extract juices and soften. Fry the cubes in the vegetable oil on low heat so that it is cooked through, soft and lightly browned.

3. **Onions:** Fry sliced onions in 2 tablespoons oil, until yellow.

4. **Tomatoes:** Add diced tomatoes to the fried onions, and let cook together for 10 minutes, until juices are released. Add the boiled chickpeas and the fried eggplant, add 1/2 teaspoon salt. Cover and cook on low for 15 minutes, until the sauce is reduced to half and no longer watery (slightly thickened).

Notes

When buying chickpeas (or dried beans in general) look for plump shiny beans with smooth skin. Beans toughen with age and will become difficult to cook. Store in a cool, dry place for no longer than one year.

To save time (and make this recipe easier), you can use canned chickpeas instead of the peeled chickpeas - still delicious.

Main Dishes

صحتين

Fatteh فتّة

Layers of Chickpeas, Beef, Yogurt, Bread, and Pine Nuts

A delicious (and somewhat addictive) multilayered dish that is easy to make.
Pay attention to the layering order so that the bread is crunchy when eaten.

Active/Total time: 30 minutes

  Serves 4

1/2 pound ground beef, 90% lean

1 tablespoon olive oil

1/2 teaspoon each salt, cinnamon, pepper

1 cup cooked chick peas, warm

2 garlic cloves, peeled

1 teaspoon salt

2/3 cup plain yogurt, stirred

1 cup, pita bread, cut into squares

1/4 cup pine nuts, toasted

1. Cook beef in olive oil breaking apart with back of spoon. Stir in 1/2 teaspoon each of salt, cinnamon and pepper.

2. Mash the garlic with 1 teaspoon salt. Transfer to a bowl and mix in the chickpeas.

3. Fry bread in 2 tablespoons of vegetable oil until crisp.

4. Just prior to serving, layer on a serving platter:

   first, the chickpeas and garlic mix,

   second, cooked beef,

   third, stirred yogurt,

   fourth, toasted pine nuts.

5. Distribute the fried bread around the layers in the serving plate. Serve and eat immediately.

1 Place garlic with salt in mortar and pestle.

2 Crush until creamy.

صحتين

Djaj bi Toom   دجاج بتوم

Garlic Chicken

Easy recipe that tastes great. Make sure you don't miss the juices in the pan.

Active time: 15 minutes   Cooking time: 45-60 minutes   Serves 4

1 pound chicken pieces, about 4-5, any kind: bone-in, boneless, skinless

10 peeled garlic cloves, crushed with 1 tablespoon of salt

1/4 cup of olive oil

1. Remove chicken from wrapping and place chicken on paper towels to drain. Trim extraneous fat.

2. Crush garlic with salt in mortar and pestle until creamy ❷. Pour the oil into the mortar and mix with the creamed garlic.

3. Spread the garlic-oil mixture on each chicken piece and place the chicken on the baking pan (preferably a pan that just fits the chicken so that the chicken doesn't dry out during baking). Repeat with all chicken pieces.

4. Bake the chicken in the oven at 400 degrees Fahrenheit, for about 30 minutes for skinless, boneless chicken, or 45-60 minutes for chicken with skin and bone. When chicken is done and juices run clear when pierced, place under broiler for 5-10 minutes to enhance color, watching carefully so that it doesn't burn.

Eat with

Pita bread, soaking up the yummy garlicky oil-juice in the pan.

1 Cook meat with pine nuts, oil, salt, cinnamon, & pepper.

2 Fry eggplant on all sides till light brown and soft.

3 Drain fried eggplant on paper towels.

4 Combine all ingredients and bake.

صحتين

Ablama Batinjan أبلما الباذنجان

Eggplant with Ground Beef

Active time: 1 hour   Cooking time: 40 minutes   Serves 4

1 pound Italian eggplant

1/2 pound ground beef

1 tablespoon pine nuts

1 tablespoon olive oil or butter

1 teaspoon salt, divided

1/4 teaspoon each cinnamon and pepper

2 tablespoon fresh lemon juice

Vegetable oil for frying eggplant

1. Peel the eggplant and cut into four equal pieces. Put the eggplant in a strainer and sprinkle 1/2 teaspoon salt on the eggplant. Let sit to release water, around 15 minutes.

2. In the meantime, put the meat in a frying pan with 1 tablespoon olive oil or butter. Add 1 teaspoon salt, the cinnamon and pepper, and pine seeds and mix well ❶. Cook on low till meat is cooked, breaking apart with back of spoon, around 10 minutes.

3. Drain eggplant and wipe dry with paper towels. Fry in 1 inch vegetable oil. Fry each piece separately and do not crowd. Fry all sides till light brown and soft ❷. Drain on paper towels ❸.

4. Line the fried eggplant in an oven safe serving dish, cover with the meat mixture, and add 1 cup hot water, and 2 tablespoons lemon juice ❹. Cover and bake at 350 degrees Fahrenheit for 30 minutes until bubbling.

Eat with

Teita's rice, plain yogurt, fresh radishes, fresh peppers.

❶ Form hamburger size patties, and place in a greased baking pan.

❷ Peel & slice the potatoes and place on top.

❸ Slice the tomatoes and place on top of the potatoes.

صحتين

Kafta bil Sayniyeh كفتة بالصينيه

Kafta in a Pan

Kafta is the name of the meat mixture: meat, parsley, and onions. Once the kafta is made, you have an option to make it into kafta in a pan (Kafta bil sayniyeh, with potatoes and tomatoes) or put it on skewers (Kafta ala syakh, Kafta on skewers) for grilling or roasting in the oven.

Active time: 1 hour   **Cooking time: 1 hour**   Serves 4

1 pound ground beef, at most 80% lean
1/2 bunch parsley, picked, washed, and minced
1 medium onion, finely chopped
1 teaspoon each salt and black pepper
2 potatoes, preferably russet
2 tomatoes, ripe but not soft
1 tablespoon tomato paste
2 tablespoon fresh lemon juice

1. **Potatoes:** Place the unpeeled potatoes in a pot and cover with water. Boil the potatoes until nearly soft. Remove the potatoes and put aside to cool. Alternatively, you can microwave the potatoes: wash well and microwave unpeeled using the power level and time recommended by your manufacturer.

2. **Kafta:** Salt and pepper the chopped onion, and mix in the chopped parsley and ground beef. Form hamburger size patties, and place in a greased baking pan ❶.

3. Place pan with kafta in 350 degrees Fahrenheit oven for 5 minutes, to partially cook. Keep oven heated.

4. Peel and slice the potatoes and place on top of the partially cooked kafta. Place a small dab of butter (about 1/2 teaspoon) on each slice and sprinkle potatoes with salt ❷.

5. **Tomatoes:** Slice the tomatoes into 1/2 inch wide slices and place on top of the potatoes ❸.

6. Dissolve the tomato paste in 1 cup hot water, add the lemon juice, and pour mixture over tomatoes, potatoes and kafta in pan.

7. Place pan in heated oven on middle rack and cook kafta until bubbling. Check that potatoes are soft and cooked through before removing. If the sauce is too diluted, leave 5 more minutes in oven to thicken.

Eat with

Teita's rice, pita bread.

صحتين

Kafta ala Syakh كفتة على سياخ

Kafta Skewers

Good for sandwiches rolled in a half pita loaf, with tarator or hommos, fresh tomatoes, mint, parsley, sliced onions with sumac, and pickled lifit.

Active time: 1 hour   Cooking time: 1 hour

 Serves 4

1 pound ground beef, at most 80% lean

1/2 bunch parsley, picked, washed, and minced

1 medium onion, finely chopped

1 teaspoon each salt and black pepper

1. If using wooden skewers, soak the skewers for 20 minutes so the wood doesn't burn during cooking.

2. Make kafta: salt and pepper the chopped onion, and mix in the chopped parsley and ground beef. Knead mixture to combine all ingredients.

3. To make the kafta skewer, take a handful of kafta and press it against a skewer, patting gently to even out thickness. If the meat does not stick and keeps falling off the skewer, it might be too wet. You can put the meat on a paper towel to remove some of the wetness and try again.

4. Grill the skewers or roast in a pan in the oven under the broil, turning to make sure all sides are done, about 5 minutes per side.

صحتين

Kibbeh كبة

Beef with Burghul and Onions

Kibbeh can be made two ways, in a pan for Kibbeh bil Sayniyeh and baked, or shaped into football-shape balls (Kibbeh Kbab) and fried. Delicious both ways. Make the base and stuffing, then choose your preparation method.

Active time: 30 minutes   Cooking time: 20 minutes

Base

1 pound ground beef, 85% lean
1 1/2 cups Burghul #1
1/2 cup diced onions
1 teaspoon salt
1/2 teaspoon pepper
1/2 teaspoon cinnamon

1. Place the burghul in a bowl. Rinse by covering with cold water, swirling by hand, draining the water, then squeezing handfuls of burghul to remove as much water as possible. Place prepared burghul in a medium bowl. Add onions, salt, pepper, cinnamon. Mix well.

2. Add meat and mix to distribute evenly. Put mixture in a food processor and process until the mixture comes together into one ball. Consistency should be soft enough to spread in a pan, but tight enough to hold shape for making kibbeh balls. If not soft enough, add cold water, one teaspoon at a time, and process again.

Stuffing

1 pound ground beef, 90% lean
2 cups diced onions
1/2 teaspoon salt
1/4 teaspoon pepper
1/4 teaspoon cinnamon
2 tablespoons olive oil
1/3 cup pine nuts

In a pan, heat oil and add onions. Sauté onions until soft and yellow, about 7 minutes, then add meat and spices, breaking up meat with back of spoon. Cook until meat is browned and all liquid is evaporated, about 10 minutes. Add pine nuts and mix. Adjust seasoning, if necessary.

1 Spread 1/2 the amount of kibbeh base on the bottom of an oiled 10-inch diameter pan.

2 Spoon the stuffing on top of the base layer, and distribute evenly.

3 Flatten small walnut-sized base in the palm of your hand, and lay gently on the stuffing.

4 Cut through the layers, making a pattern of diagonals or squares.

Kibbeh bil Sayniyeh   كبه بالصينيه

Kibbeh in a Pan

Active time: 45 minutes   **Baking time: 30-40 minutes**    **Serves 4**

1. Spread 1/2 the amount of kibbeh base on the bottom of an oiled 10-inch diameter pan, or similar final area ❶. Flatten by hand to even thickness.

2. Spoon the stuffing on top of the base layer, and distribute evenly ❷.

3. Flatten small walnut-sized base in the palm of your hand, and lay gently on the stuffing ❸. Continue till you cover all the stuffing. Dip fingers in cold water or olive oil, and rub over the top layer to connect the pieces, flatten, and smooth the edges.

4. With a sharp knife, cut through the layers, making a pattern of diagonals or squares, so that the oil can penetrate and cook all the layers of kibbeh ❹.

5. Spread 1 tablespoon olive oil on top layer, divide 2 tablespoons of butter over the pan.

6. Bake on middle rack at 400 degrees Fahrenheit, for 30 minutes until edges are browned and bubbling. Move the pan to the top rack and broil for a few minutes to get a nice color.

Note

Burghul is made from wheat groats that are picked, boiled until the kernel breaks open, drained and put to dry. The dried wheat is taken to a mill to grind into coarse, medium, and fine burghul, each for a different use. The finest ground, #1, for tabbouleh and kibbeh, medium ground #2 for burghul bi banadoora, and #3 coarsest ground (not used in the recipes in this book) can be used in dishes that require long cooking times.

Eat with

Plain yogurt or a salad.

1 Poke a hole in the center of the walnut and push through the length of the kibbeh.

2 Press down against the palm, while turning the kibbeh until you get a thickness of 1/16th of an inch wall.

3 Put a teaspoon of stuffing in the hollow of the ball.

4 Bring the edges together to seal the opening by making an "O" shape with your right index and thumb.

5 Turn the kibbeh while closing the opening.

6 Shape the sealed end to match the other end.

7 Finished kibbeh ball.

8 Fried kibbeh balls.

Kibbeh Kbab كبه كباب

Kibbeh Balls

Active time: 1.5 hours   **Frying time: 45 minutes**   **Makes 20-30 depending on size**

Making the kibbeh balls:

1. Wet your left palm with cold water.

2. Take a walnut-size piece of kibbeh base, place the kibbeh in your left palm, in a cupping position.

3. Using your index finger, poke a hole in the center of the walnut and push through the length of the kibbeh ❶.

4. Hollow out the ball with your right index finger, pressing down against the palm, while turning the kibbeh. As the walls of the kibbeh get thinner and the kibbeh lengthens, try to keep the thickness of the walls even. You should get an opening of about 1.5 inches with a thickness of 1/16th of an inch wall ❷. The kibbeh ball should be about 3 inches long, with a tapered end.

5. Put a teaspoon of stuffing in the hollow of the ball ❸.

6. Bring the edges together to seal the opening by making an "O" shape with your right index and thumb, and turn the kibbeh while closing the opening to shape the sealed end to match the other end ❹❺❻, finally pressing closed to make the football shape ❼.

7. Deep fry kibbeh in vegetable oil. Use enough oil to cover the kibbeh balls. Place them gently in the hot oil so they don't splatter. Fry in batches, without crowding. Turn for even color, about 4-5 minutes per side. Remove with slotted spoon or spatula and place on plate lined with paper towels to absord the extra oil. Serve hot or at room temperature ❽.

Eat with

Yogurt, hommos, baba ghnouj, tabbouleh.

1 Foam rising to the surface.

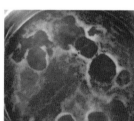

2 After the foam is skimmed off.

3 Store in mason jars for a portable lunch.

صحتين

Yakhnet Bamyah يخنة باميه

Okra Stew

Easy when you use frozen okra.

Active time: 30 minutes   Cooking time: 1 hour

Serves 4

1 pound stew meat, cubed

1 onion, chopped

2 tablespoons olive oil

6 garlic cloves, peeled, each cut in half crosswise

1 pound frozen okra, sliced or whole

2 ripe tomatoes, diced, or two tablespoons tomato paste dissolved in half cup hot water

1 bunch fresh cilantro, picked, washed, chopped

1. In a saucepan, boil 3 cups water, add the meat, and bring back to boil. Skim off the foam (① with foam, ② after foam skimmed off). Let it boil for 30 minutes at low heat, until the water is reduced to one cup, and the meat is cooked (when you can easily insert a fork in the meat). Remove the meat and save the broth.

2. In a fry pan, cook the onion and garlic in 2 tablespoons of olive oil, until soft. Add the meat, okra, tomatoes, cilantro, salt, and black pepper, and cook on low heat for 15 minutes. Mix gently. Add the broth, about 1 cup, to cover all the ingredients. If not enough, add water, about 1/2 cup. If using tomato paste, add it now. Cook for 10 more minutes, until the okra is soft. Season to taste with salt.

Eat with

Teita's rice, fresh radishes.

Note

All the stews are great for packing the night before in a microwave-safe jar and taking to work for a delicious hot lunch the next day . Just uncover, pop in the microwave, and enjoy.

1 Foam rising to the surface.

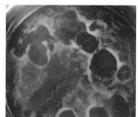

2 After the foam is skimmed off.

صحتين

Yakhnet Bazella   يخنة باز لاء

Sweet Pea Stew

Good with either frozen or fresh green peas.

Active time: 30 minutes   Cook time: 1 hour   Serves 6

1 **pound stew meat, cubed**

1 **pound green peas**

1 **onion, chopped**

2 **tablespoons olive oil**

6 **garlic cloves, whole**

2 **ripe tomatoes, diced, or two tablespoons tomato paste dissolved in half cup hot water**

1 **bunch fresh cilantro, picked, washed, chopped**

1. In a saucepan, boil 3 cups water, add the meat, and bring back to boil. Skim off the foam . Then let it boil for 30 minutes at low heat, until the water is reduced to one cup, and the meat cooked (can easily insert a fork in the meat) ❷. Remove the meat and save the broth.

2. In a fry pan, cook the onion and garlic in 2 tablespoons olive oil, until soft. Add the meat with the green peas, tomatoes, cilantro, salt, black pepper, and cook on low heat for 15 minutes. Add the broth, about 1 cup, to cover all the ingredients. If not enough, add boiling water, about 1/2 cup. If using tomato paste, add it now. Cook on low for 10 more minutes, until the green peas are soft. Season to taste.

Eat with

Teita's rice, fresh radishes.

1 Foam rising to the surface.

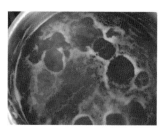

2 After foam is skimmed off.

صحتين

Yakhnet Loubyeh يخنة لوبيه

Green Bean Stew

Easy and healthy - good with either frozen or fresh green beans.

Active time: 30 minutes   **Cooking time: 1 hour**   Serves 6

1 pound stew meat, cubed

1 pound green beans

1 onion, chopped

2 tablespoons olive oil

6 garlic cloves, peeled, each cut in half crosswise

2 ripe tomatoes, diced, or two tablespoons tomato paste dissolved in half cup hot water

1 bunch fresh cilantro, picked, washed, chopped

Note

Preparing fresh green beans: Cut both tips and break each bean in half. Rinse beans with fresh water before using.

You can also use frozen green beans. Thaw the beans and break each bean into two inch long pieces before using.

1. In a saucepan, boil 3 cups water, add the meat, and bring back to boil. Skim off the foam . Then let it boil for 30 minutes at low heat, until the water is reduced to one cup, and the meat is cooked (test by checking that you can easily insert a fork in the meat) ❷. Remove the meat and save the broth.

2. In a fry pan, cook the onions and garlic in 2 tablespoons olive oil, until soft. Add the cooked meat with the green beans, tomatoes, cilantro, salt, black pepper, and cook on low heat for 15 minutes. Add the broth, about 1 cup, to cover all the ingredients. If using tomato paste, add it now. Cook for 10 more minutes, until the green beans are soft. Season to taste with salt and pepper.

Eat with

Teita's rice, fresh radishes.

صحتين

Yakhnet Sabanekh يخنة سبانخ

Spinach Stew

Active time: 15 minutes   Total time: 45 minutes

 Serves 4

1 pound chopped spinach, fresh or frozen

1/2 pound ground beef, at least 90% lean

1 onion, chopped

1 tablespoon olive oil

3/4 cup cilantro, chopped and washed

1 teaspoon each salt and pepper, divided

1. If using fresh spinach in a bunch, chop the leaves and keep one inch of the stems close to the leaves. Discard the rest of the stalks and roots. Wash in water three times to remove visible sand/sediment. Put in a colander to drain for 5 minutes.

   If using prewashed baby spinach, it's ready to go out of the container - just needs chopping.

2. Sauté the chopped onions in olive oil until soft. Add the beef and brown, breaking apart with back of spoon. Season with 1/2 teaspoon each salt and pepper.

3. Add the spinach and cilantro, mix to distribute evenly. Sprinkle the other 1/2 teaspoon each of salt and pepper. Cover and cook on low until spinach is wilted and cooked through, around 20 minutes. If the spinach does not produce enough juice to cook, you can add 1/4 cup of water.

Eat with

Teita's rice and a squeeze of fresh lemon juice.

1 Foam rising to the surface.

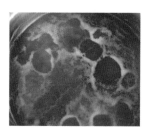

2 After the foam is skimmed off.

Yakhnet Fassoulia يخنة فاصولية
Dried Broad Bean Stew

Active time: 30 minutes   **Cook time: 1 hour**   Serves 4

Advance planning: beans need to be soaked overnight

1 pound stew meat, cubed

1/2 pound dried broad beans

1 onion, chopped

2 tablespoons olive oil

6 garlic cloves, peeled, each cut into 4 pieces

2 tablespoons tomato paste

1 bunch fresh cilantro, picked, washed, chopped

1. The night before, soak dried beans in water. Put the beans in a large bowl, and cover the beans with clean water to 2 inches above the level of the beans. Cover and let sit on counter overnight.

2. Next day, drain the beans. Place the beans in a saucepan with enough water to cover 2 inches above level of beans. Boil the beans until they are soft, and the skin cracks. Drain and set aside.

3. In a saucepan, boil 3 cups water, add the stew meat, and boil. Skim off the foam . Then let it simmer for 30 minutes at low heat, until the water is reduced to one cup, and the meat is cooked (can easily insert a fork in the meat). Remove the meat and save the beef broth.

4. In a fry pan, sauté the onions and garlic in 2 tablespoons of olive oil, until soft. Add the meat with the cooked beans, cilantro, salt, black pepper, and cook on low heat for 5 minutes.

5. Add the beef broth, about 1 cup, to cover all the ingredients. If the broth is not enough, add water, about 1/2 cup.

6. Dissolve the tomato paste in a cup of hot water, and add to pot. Cook for 10 more minutes, until the sauce thickens. Season to taste.

Eat with

Teita's rice, fresh radishes.

1 Add crushed garlic and sauté until fragrant.

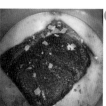

2 Add the chopped molokhia.

3 Boil 3 minutes only.

4 Pickled onion dressing.

صحتين

Molokhia ملوخية

Jews Mallow Stew

This meal has five parts, rice, chicken, molokhia, bread, pickled onions,
all of which you can layer onto your plate in any order you want.

Active time: 30 minutes   Cooking time: 1 hour

Serves 4

2 pounds molokhia leaves (called Jews mallow, or jute plant), washed, drained and chopped. This recipe uses frozen chopped molokhia available at Middle Eastern markets - use a 16-ounce packet.

2 pounds chicken pieces, any kind

1 onion, chopped

2 tablespoons butter

1 tablespoon peeled garlic, crushed with 1 teaspoon salt

1 tablespoon coriander powder

2 tablespoons lemon juice

1 tablespoon apple cider vinegar

1/2 tsp black pepper

1/2 tsp cinnamon

1 loaf of pita bread, toasted and broken into bite-size pieces

1. **Chicken:** Boil enough water to cover the chicken. Add chicken, two bay leaves, 5 whole peppercorns, 2 cardamom pods.

Bring to a boil and cook on medium heat until done, about 30 minutes. Remove chicken and reserve broth. Remove chicken skin and debone if necessary, and shred the chicken by hand for serving. Sprinkle with pepper and cinnamon.

2. **Molokhia:** Sauté onion in 2 tablespoons of butter, until onion is yellow. Add crushed garlic and sauté until fragrant . Add coriander powder, chicken broth, 2 tablespoons lemon juice, 1 tablespoon vinegar, and bring to a boil. Just before serving, add the chopped molokhia ❷, and boil 3 minutes only ❸ – boiling longer will turn the molokhia black.

3. **Onions:** For the pickled onion dressing, combine 1 onion finely chopped, 1/4 teaspoon salt, 1 cup apple cider vinegar or enough to cover the onion ❹. Let sit for 30 minutes to pickle onions.

Eat with

Rice, passing the toasted pita bread on the side

صحتين

Mjadra مجدرة

Lentil Stew

Good hot for a warm winter meal or cold for a refreshing meal in the summer.

Active & cooking time total: 4 hours   VG Serves 4

**1 cup dried whole lentils, picked and rinsed
  with water**
2 cups onion, chopped
1/3 cup white rice
1/2 cup olive oil
1/2 tablespoon salt, divided

Notes

Use large green lentils in this recipe.

You can reduce 1 hour cooking time by soaking the lentils in water the night before.

A pressure cooker would save time here, too. If using, you can add the caramelized onions, uncooked lentils, rice, and 4 cups water. Cover and cook according to manufacturer directions.

1. Rinse lentils in water, drain and put in a medium size pot. Add 4 cups water and bring to boil on low heat. Simmer for about 1 3/4 hours, until lentils crack and are soft.

2. In a separate pan, fry the onion in 1/2 cup olive oil till caramelized, and dark brown in color, about 20 minutes.

3. While onions are frying, wash the rice: put rice in a bowl, cover with water, stir gently with your hand, and pour out as much as possible of the cloudy water.

4. Add the rice and the caramelized onions to the hot lentils. Add 1 cup boiling water. Simmer, stirring often, until the mixture is thick, the consistency of pudding, about 30 minutes. Be sure to stir often so that the rice doesn't stick to the bottom of the pan. If necessary, add more water to continue cooking the rice - you want to cook the rice until you can no longer see a complete grain. When cooked through, add salt.

5. Pour the mjadra in a food processor and purée until creamy.

Eat with

Yogurt, salad, green onions, pickled vegetables.

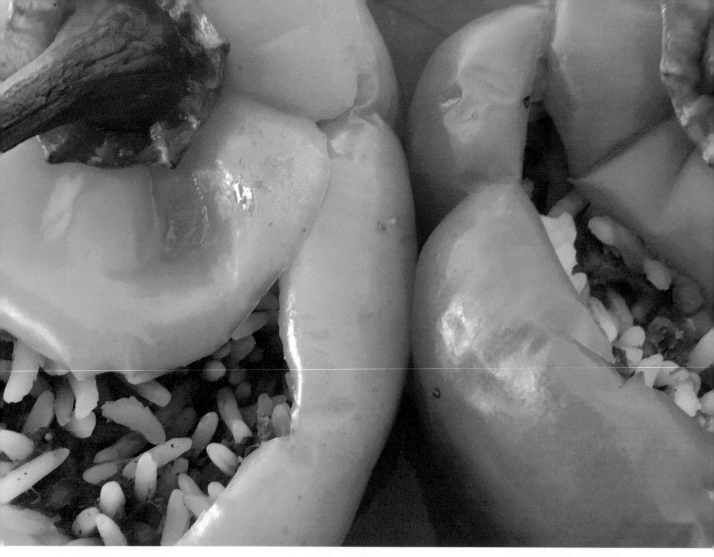

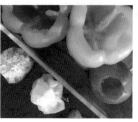

1 Trim seeds from top and inside of pepper.

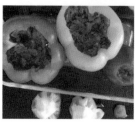

2 Fill pepper with the prepared stuffing.

3 Pour dissolved tomato paste liquid.

صحتين

Flayfleh Mihshiyeh ma'a Banadoora فليفله محشيه مع بندورة

Stuffed Sweet Bell Peppers

Use all the colors of peppers for a colorful dish.

Active time: 30 minutes   Baking time: 45 minutes   Serves 3

3 fresh bell peppers, one of each color, yellow, red, green, about three
1 cup white rice
1 teaspoon salt, divided
1/2 teaspoon black pepper
1/4 teaspoon cinnamon
1/2 pound ground beef, 90% lean
1/4 cup vegetable oil
2 heaping tablespoons tomato paste dissolved in 2 cups hot water

Make the stuffing:

1. Put the rice in a medium bowl, cover with water, and swirl gently with your hand. Drain the rice by tilting the bowl gently and catching any falling rice grains with your other hand.

2. Place the drained rice in a bowl, add 1/2 teaspoon salt, black pepper, and cinnamon and mix. Add 1/4 cup oil and ground beef, and mix well.

Prepare the peppers:

3. Cut 1-inch rim of pepper around the green stem. Remove tops to use later. Using a knife, trim the seeds from the top of the pepper and from inside the pepper ❶. Place peppers in an oven-safe dish or pyrex appropriate for serving.

Line up peppers in a tight arrangement so that they don't expand too much when cooked. If you have additional space but can't fit a pepper, add a tomato to stuff along with the peppers (If using tomoato, arrange top down, cut a two inch circle from the bottom to core the tomato. You can save the cores to add with the tomato paste during cooking. Stuff the tomato and replace the cut circle to cover).

4. Fill 3/4 of the cored peppers with the prepared stuffing . Don't overfill.

5. Dissolve tomato paste in 1/2 cup boiling water, then add the rest of the 2 cups hot water to the tomato paste mixture.

6. Cover peppers with cut tops. Pour tomato paste liquid onto peppers 3/4 of the way up the dish ❸. Sprinkle 1/2 teaspoon salt on the peppers.

7. Cover with foil and place in the oven at 425 degrees Fahrenheit for about 30 minutes. The peppers are done when they are soft and the rice is cooked.

Eat with

Fresh radishes.

① Score
deeply
around the
core.

② Remove
about 2
iches of the
core.

③ Leaves soft
and pliable
for rolling.

صحتين

Mihshi Malfoof محشي ملفوف

Stuffed Cabbage

Garlic lover's meal. Whole unpeeled cloves of garlic are thrown in the pot along with the rolled cabbage for flavor, but the garlic itself is the special treat since it comes out creamy and succulent.

Active time: 30 minutes   Cooking time: 30-40 minutes   Serves 4

1 cabbage, about 3 pounds, preferably white cabbage. Green cabbage will work, though the leaves are a bit tougher and will take longer to soften enough for rolling.
1/2 pound ground beef
2/3 cup rice
1/4 teaspoon salt and pepper each
2 tablespoons olive oil
10 cloves garlic, unpeeled, loose white outer peel removed.

Note

Very important, choose a cabbage that is more flat than spherical, with narrow leaf ribs and the leaves not very tightly packed. Doesn't matter if the outside leaves are green or white, but stay away from the ones with black marks or mold.

1. **Prepare the cabbage:** Core cabbage by scoring deeply around the core with a knife and remove the core ❶. If difficult to remove, you can remove it after microwaving the whole cabbage on "Fresh Vegetable" setting. Pull out about 2 inches of the core ❷.

To soften the cabbage leaves for rolling:

Method 1: Cut off the cabbage leaves at the core, and try to pull the leaves off one at a time. If they tear, it's OK, as long as you end up with a piece large enough to roll. In a large pot, boil enough water to submerge cabbage leaves. Place two or three cabbage leaves in the boiling water to soften, about 5 minutes. Remove the leaves into a bowl. Allow to cool before rolling.

Method 2: Place the whole cabbage in the microwave after scoring around the core. Microwave on "Fresh Vegetable" setting until the leaves come off easily, about 5 minutes. If you haven't removed the core, check the cabbage after the first 2.5 minutes and pull out the core. After 5 minutes in the microwave, remove the cabbage. Once cool enough to touch, separate as many cabbage leaves as possible. If needed, put the leaves back in the microwave again, another 2.5 minutes, or as much as needed in order to make the leaves soft and pliable for rolling ❸. Be careful when removing leaves after microwaving – they will be hot.

1 Add meat to the seasoned rice and mix.

2 Place garlic in the bottom of the saucepan.

3 Slice the rib of the cabbage leaf.

4 Spead stuffing from rib edge to cover the length of the leaf.

5 Roll leaf, leaving no stuffing exposed.

6 Place the rolled cabbage leaf seam down in the prepared pan.

7 Add lemon juice and mint to peeled garlic to make the topping.

8 Pour the topping on top of the cabbage in the pan.

2. **Prepare the stuffing:** Place the rice in a medium bowl, cover with cold water, swirl gently with your hand a few times, then drain rice by tilting the bowl gently to once side, allowing the cloudy water to pour out while catching falling rice grains with your other hand. Add 1/4 teaspoon each of salt and pepper and mix into rice. Add the oil and mix gently. Add the meat and mix **1**.

3. Prior to rolling, prepare the saucepan you will be using for cooking the rolled cabbage leaves. Place the garlic in the bottom of a saucepan **2**.

4. **To roll:** spread the cabbage leaf on a flat surface, and slice off the rib. You will have two pieces of cabbage leaf **3**. You may have to cut each half again so that the rolled cabbage leaf fits in your pan. Line up the pieces longitudinally, arranging the leaf with the rib part closest to you. Place a small amount of stuffing on the rib edge of the leaf and spread it to the length of the leaf **4**. Roll the leaf starting from the rib edge. Make sure that none of the stuffing is exposed **5**. Place the rolled cabbage leaf seam side down in the prepared pan **6**.

5. Continue rolling and piling the leaves in the pan in a tight layered arrangement. As you get to the smaller leaves, you may not need to cut the leaf in half, and the rib may be soft enough to roll. Use an amount of meat mixture that is proportional to the size of the leaf. Depending on the number of leaves, and the size of the leaves, you may have stuffing left over. You can freeze it and use it for stuffing sweet peppers, coussa, grape leaves, etc.

6. Put the pan on the stove and sprinkle the rolled cabbage with some salt. Cover the cabbage with boiling water. Bring to boil on high heat and boil for 5 minutes. Lower heat to medium and continue cooking for 30 minutes.

Topping:
3 peeled garlic cloves
1 tablespoon fresh lemon juice
1 teaspoon dried mint

7. **Prepare topping:** Crush peeled garlic with salt until creamy. Add lemon juice and dried mint, and mix **7**.

8. Once the cabbage is cooked, pour the topping on top of the cabbage in the pan **8**. Let cook for 5-7 minutes longer. It's ready when the cabbage is soft and the meat and rice are cooked.

Eat with

Squeeze of fresh lemon juice, fresh radishes.

Note

You will probably have the heart of the cabbage left over - you can use it for making burghul bi banadoora (p.43).

صحتين

Djaj Mihshi دجاج محشي

Chicken Stuffed with Rice and Nuts

This is a special dish, served at family holiday events and gatherings.

Active time: 1 hour   Cooking time: 2 hours

Serves 4

One whole chicken, about 5 pounds

1/2 pound ground beef, at least 85% lean

1 tablespoon vegetable oil

1 cup rice, washed and drained

1/4 cup pine nuts

1/4 cup blanched almonds (almonds without the peel)

1 teaspoon salt

1/2 teaspoon each cinnamon, black pepper, and ground nutmeg.

1-2 tablespoons plain yogurt

1. **Seasoning mixture:** Mix 1 teaspoon salt, 1/2 teaspoon each cinnamon, black pepper, and ground nutmeg. Prepare two portions of the seasoning mixture and set aside.

2. **Chicken:** Clean chicken, removing the chicken giblets from inside chicken, rinse inside and outside chicken with cold water. Using paper towels, dry inside and outside of chicken well.

3. Prepare the roasting pan. Line pan with pieces of foil long enough to wrap the chicken. Alternatively, you can use an oven bag.

4. Place the chicken in the prepared pan. Spread one quantity of the seasoning mixture over the inside and outside of the chicken (❶ on following page). Set chicken aside as you prepare the stuffing.

1 Spread one quantity of the seasoning mixture over the inside and outside of the chicken.

2 Roast nuts until golden.

3 Add the roasted nuts to the cool stuffing.

4 Spoon the stuffing into the chicken.

5 Spread a tablespoon of plain yogurt on the outside of the stuffed chicken.

5. **Stuffing:** Wash rice. Place the rice in a medium bowl, cover with cold water, swirl gently with your hand a few times, then drain rice by tilting the bowl gently to one side, allowing the cloudy water to pour out while catching falling rice grains with your other hand.

6. In a medium saucepan, sauté the beef in vegetable oil over low heat until cooked through and all the water has evaporated.

7. Add the rice and the second seasoning mixture portion, and mix well. Add 1 1/4 cup of boiling water or hot chicken broth. Cover and cook for 30 minutes, until the rice is cooked and the water is absorbed. Let cool.

8. **Nuts:** Place nuts on a baking sheet in the oven under the broiler for one minute, until golden ❷. Note that the pine nuts will roast faster than the almonds so it's best to put them in separate pans to ensure proper roasting. Alternatively, you can fry the nuts in vegetable oil. If you do, keep an eye out so they don't burn, and drain excess oil by placing the nuts on paper towels. Add the roasted nuts to the cool stuffing ❸.

9. Before stuffing the chicken, make sure to dry the chicken again: the seasoning on the chicken will cause the chicken to produce moisture.

10. Spoon the stuffing into the chicken ❹. You will have stuffing left over which you can serve on the side.

11. Spread a tablespoon of plain yogurt on the outside of the stuffed chicken ❺. Wrap the stuffed chicken with foil and place in a roasting pan. Bake on the center rack, at 425 degrees Fahrenheit for 15 minutes, then reduce the temperature to 350 degrees Fahrenheit and bake the chicken for 20 minutes/pound, or about 1.5 hours, or until cooked (the juices run clear when pierced) and the skin is golden brown. Remove from oven and let rest covered for 15 minutes.

Eat with

Plain yogurt or salad.

1 Place stuffed squash in a saucepan.

2 Simmer for 30 minutes til squash is soft & juice is reduced by half.

Coussa Mihshi ma'a Banadoora كوسا محشي مع بندورة

Stuffed Coussa Squash with Tomato Sauce

Active time: 30 minutes   Cooking time: 45 minutes   Serves 4

1 1/2 pounds coussa squash, a type of summer squash. Other types of squash can be used, cut to adjust the length so you can core it.
1 cup white rice
1/2 pound ground beef, 90% lean
1 teaspoon each salt and pepper
1/4 teaspoon cinnamon
2 tablespoons tomato paste
2 tablespoons olive oil

1. **Stuffing:** Wash the rice in cold water: place the rice in a medium bowl, cover with cold water, swirl gently with your hand a few times, then drain by tilting the bowl, allowing the water to pour out one side while catching falling rice grains with your other hand. Add salt, black pepper, and cinnamon to the drained rice and mix. Add olive oil and ground beef, and mix well.

2. **Squash:** Rinse squash in clean water. Cut off the top stem. Core with coussa corer to make room for stuffing (see next page for coring directions). Rinse cored interior of squash with cold water and drain.

3. Stuff the squash with the rice/meat stuffing leaving one inch from the top for rice to expand.

4. Place stuffed squash in a saucepan ❶.

5. Dissolve tomato paste in 2 cups hot water. Pour tomato paste mixture onto squash to cover.

6. Sprinkle 1/2 teaspoon salt on squash and boil covered on stovetop for 15 minutes then let simmer for 30 minutes until juice is reduced by half and the squash is soft enough for a fork to penetrate easily .

1 Make three cuts around the tip in a circle formation.

2 Remove the core by inserting & twisting the corer.

3 Slide the corer out, removing the core.

4 Continue scraping the inner walls until rim is about 1/4 inch.

Note

Coring squash: Place the squash in the palm of your left hand with the cut tip exposed. With the corer in your right hand, insert the corer into the cut end of the squash and make three arcs inside the rim in a circle formation to set the outside coring lines **1**. Remove the core of the squash by inserting and twisting the corer, and then sliding the corer out **2**. The corer should contain parts of the squash core **3**. Remove the core from the corer and continue coring and scraping the inner walls of the squash until you have a rim of about 1/4 inch, or enough room to stuff the squash **4**. Make sure to not damage the bottom and side walls of the squash. If you do, no worries, you can now use the squash for the Na'rat Coussa recipe. Once you are done coring, remove the small brown base of the squash.

Coussa Mihshi wa Warak Aareesh

كوسا محشي و ورق عريش

Stuffed Coussa Squash and Stuffed Grape Leaves

Active time: 1 hour   Cooking time: 45 -60 minutes   Serves 4

1 1/2 pounds of squash (around 6)

20 grape leaves

1 pound ground beef, 90% lean

2 cups white rice

1/2 cup olive oil

1 teaspoon salt

1/2 teaspoon pepper

1/2 teaspoon cinnamon

1 tablespoon butter

2 tablespoons lemon juice

1. **Stuffing:** Wash the rice in cold water: place the rice in a medium bowl, cover with cold water, swirl gently with your hand a few times, then drain by tilting the bowl, allowing the water to pour out one side while catching falling rice grains with your other hand.

2. To the rice, add salt and pepper, cinnamon and oil, and mix. Add the meat and mix well.

3. **Squash:** Core the squash and remove the seeds and pulp so that the remaining squash wall is approximately 1/8 inch. You want to make sure that the opening in the squash for stuffing is large enough to insert the meat/rice mixture without creating an air bubble inside the squash .

4. Rinse the cored squash to remove any leftover pulp and drain before stuffing.

5. Stuff the cored squash leaving an inch on top for the expansion of the rice in cooking. Arrange in a pot large enough to handle the squash and the grape leaves.

1 Place stuffing in the middle of the leaf, at the widest part of the leaf, in the shape of a small log as wide as your finger.

2 To roll, fold in the two leaf edges, right and left.

3 Layer the rolled grape leaves on top of the squash in the pot, arranging in a tight pattern.

6. **Grape leaves:** If fresh from the vine, choose the green, tender, flexible leaves for easy rolling, about the size of the palm of your hand. Remove the stem. Soak in warm water to wilt, about 1 minute, and remove to a colander to drain.

   If from a jar, rinse the leaves from the salt solution, and drain. Remove stem with a pair of scissors prior to rolling.

7. To roll, spread one grape leaf on a surface, shiny side down, with the stem edge closest to you. Place stuffing in the middle of the leaf, at the widest part of the leaf, in the shape of a small log as wide as your finger ❶. Make sure to leave about 1/3 of the leaf on either side of the stuffing. To roll, fold in the two leaf edges, right and left ❷, and then roll from the stem edge away from you toward the tip of the grape leaf, making a tight roll.

8. Layer the rolled grape leaves on top of the squash in the pot, arranging in a tight pattern ❸.

9. Put small slices of the butter on the grape leaves. Sprinkle some salt and pepper on top, then pour on the lemon juice.

10. Cover the surface of the grape leaves with an upside down plate or saucer to prevent the leaves from floating when adding water. Pour boiling water on top to just cover the rolled grape leaves and squash.

11. Cover pot and boil on high heat for 5 minutes, then reduce to medium heat and simmer for 30 minutes.

Eat with

Garlic yogurt (2 cups plain yogurt, 1 clove peeled garlic, crushed with 1/2 teaspoon of salt).

Baked Specialties

صحتين

Mana'eesh bi Zaa'tar مناقيش

Zaa'tar Pastry

The word "mana'eesh" is the plural of "man'ousheh", a special breakfast treat with zaa'tar.

Active time: 45 minutes   **2 dough proofings 30-45 minutes**
Baking time: 35 minutes

Makes 10

5 cups flour
2 tablespoons vegetable oil
11/4 tablespoons salt
1 cup each water and milk
2 teaspoons dry yeast
1 teaspoon sugar
5 tablespoons zaa'tar
9 tablespoons olive oil

Dough

1. Combine flour, vegetable oil, and salt in a mixing bowl. Mix well.

2. Add yeast and sugar to warm water (hot but still tolerable to touch - 40 degrees Centigrade, 100 degrees Farenheit) and let sit for 10 minutes to activate and get foamy. Add activated yeast to flour mixture. Use one cup milk to rinse the yeast cup and add to the mixing bowl.

3. Knead or mix (with dough hook if using an electric mixer) until dough is no longer sticky to your fingers, adding flour as needed, a tablespoon at a time. Let sit covered to proof in a warm spot until doubled in size, around 30-45 minutes.

Zaa'tar Mix

1. In a small bowl, mix zaa'tar with olive oil. ①

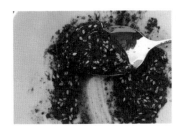

① zaa'tar mixed with olive oil.

Note

Zaa'tar is made from the flower of the Middle Eastern wild thyme (*Thymus capitatus*). After drying, the flowers are ground to a powder, and mixed with salt and sumac. For every pound of zaa'tar flowers, a 1/2 pound of sumac and a 1/4 cup kosher salt is added. Finally, a 1/2 pound toasted sesame seeds is mixed in. Zaa'tar from other Middle Eastern countries might include one or more other spice such as cumin, fennel, caraway, oregano, garlic powder, coriander, anise.

1

On a clean surface, roll dough ball into a log 16 inches long and about 2.5 inches in diameter.

2

Separate log into eight equal segments.

3

Tuck edges down to create rounded mounds.

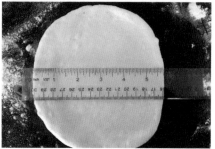

4

Roll out into disks.

5

Place disks on cookie sheet lined in parchment paper.

6

After 30-45 minutes dough begins to rise and small bubble form across the disk.

7

Tamp down each disk about 8 times with a spoon to prevent the center rising.

8

Bake until disks are firm and bottoms are browned.

صحتين

Mana'eesh bi Zaa'tar مناقيش

Zaa'tar Pastry - Continued

Zaa'tar is believed to enhance memory and so, Lebanese students make sure to each a manoushe before a test to improve performance.

Roll out Dough Disks

1. Clean and dry working surface. Use flour to prevent dough from sticking while rolling.

2. Roll dough ball into a log 16 inches long and 2.5 inches in diameter ❶. Separate into 8 equal segments of dough ❷.

3. Take each piece of dough and tuck the edges down into a single point (this will be the center of the back of each disk). Roll the gathered ends between your hands to smooth into a thin log and tuck into the rest of the dough, making a rounded mound ❸.

4. With flour and a rolling pin, roll mounds into disks 5-6 inches in diameter ❹. Place on a cookie sheet lined with parchment paper ❺. Let sit for 30-45 minutes to proof again, until dough begins to rise and small bubbles begin to form across each disk ❻.

Baking

1. Preheat oven to 400 degrees Fahrenheit.

2. Spread a scant tablespoon of zaa'tar mixture on each disk using a spoon, leaving a clear 1/2 inch edge. Tamp down each disk by pressing down (without poking through the bottom of the disk) with the edge of the spoon, about 8 tamps spread over the zaa'tar area ❼.

3. Place baking sheet in center rack of oven, bake for 15-17 minutes, until disks are firm to touch and bottoms are browned ❽. Best eaten warm.

Note

For storing, stack the mana'eesh, two at a time with the zaa'tar sides together ❽, wrap in foil, and place in a plastic bag in the fridge or freezer. Let thaw and/or toast slightly before enjoying.

Eat with

Cut cucumbers, hot tea, sliced cheese, labneh.

Fatayer bi Sabanekh فطاير بي سبانخ

Spinach Triangles

This appetizer takes some time to prepare, but worth the trouble. The secret is making sure to squeeze as much of the spinach juice from the fresh spinach as possible.

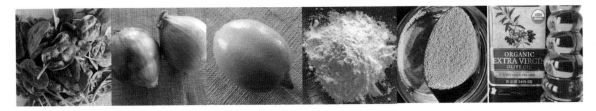

Active: 1.5 hours   Inactive: 1 hour   Baking time: 30 minutes   **Makes 25-30 pieces**

Dough

3 cups all purpose flour
1 teaspoon dry yeast, soaked in 1/2 cup warm water, hot but still tolerable to the touch (40 degrees Centigrade, 100 degrees Fahrenheit)
3 tablespoons olive oil
About 1 cup water
3/4 teaspoon salt
Vegetable oil for the baking pan

1. Add yeast in warm water and let stand to activate and foam, about 10 minutes.

2. In a mixing bowl, combine flour, salt and olive oil. Add foamy yeast, and then enough water to bring the dough together (about 1 cup). Knead the dough until smooth, 5 mintues.

3. Let sit covered in a warm spot to rise, about 30 minutes. In the meantime, prepare spinach filling and baking pan.

Spinach Filling

2/3 pound fresh baby spinach
1 1/2 teaspoon each salt, black pepper, and chili pepper
1/2 cup yellow onion, finely chopped
4 tablespoons fresh lemon juice
2 tablespoons olive oil

1. If in a bunch, chop the leaves and keep one inch of the stems close to the leaves. Discard the rest of the stalks and roots. Wash in water three times to remove visible sand/sediment. Put in colander to drain for 5 minutes. If using prewashed baby spinach, it's ready to go out of the container - just needs chopping.

2. Put the chopped spinach in a bowl, sprinkle with 1 teaspoon salt, and mix well. Leave for 15 minutes to wilt to half the volume.

① Prepared spinach filling.

② Cut dough rounds & place 1 teaspoon of filling.

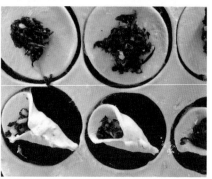

③ Bring in two sides.

④ Bring up last part to center line, seal to make triangle.

صحتين

Spinach Filling (continued)

3. Take handfuls of spinach and squeeze out all liquid/juice. Continue squeezing until no more juice squeezes out.

4. Add chopped onion to squeezed spinach, along with 1/2 teaspoon salt, 1/2 teaspoon pepper, 1/2 teaspoon chili pepper, 4 tablespoons fresh lemon juice, 2 tablespoons olive oil, and mix well. Taste for additional salt or lemon.

Assembly & Baking

1. Prepare the cookie sheet. Pour 2 tablespoons vegetable oil on cookie sheet. No need to spread the oil now since you will be dipping the tops of the triangles in the oil prior to placing the triangles on the cookie sheet.

2. Once the dough has risen, take dough out, and divide into thirds. Roll out each third to 1/8 inch thick, and cut 3-inch diameter rounds with a cookie cutter, a glass rim, etc ❷.

3. Put 1 rounded teaspoon of prepared spinach filling ❶ on center of each round ❷. To make a spinach triangle, take two sides of the circle and seal 2/3 of the way down to make a center seal, and one corner of the triangle ❸. Then bring up last part of the circle, and seal against the center line to make the two additional corners, making a triangle ❹.

4. Oil the top of the spinach triangle by passing the top of the spinach triangle in the oil on the cookie sheet. Line the spinach triangles on the cookie sheet.

5. Let the triangles rest in the pan for 10 minutes. Bake in oven at 350 degrees Fahrenheit, on center rack for about 20 minutes, or until bottoms and tops are light brown.

6. Remove from oven. Let cool on pan.

Eat with

Feta Cheese.

Lahmeh bi Ajin لحمه بي عجين

Meat and Nut Pastry

The dough in this recipe is made paper-thin by hand. As a time saving alternative you can use Filo dough, just make sure to butter all the layers as you fold them to make the dough base.

Active time: 1.5 hours Baking time: 30 minutes

 Makes 20

Filling:

1/2 white onion, diced

1/4 pound 90% lean ground beef

1 tablespoon vegetable oil

1 teaspoon cinnamon

1 teaspoon each salt & pepper

3 tablespoons pine nuts

2 tablespoons plain yogurt

1. Heat vegetable oil in a skillet over medium-high heat. Add onions and sauté until soft and transparent.

2. Add ground beef to skillet and fry until cooked through and juices evaporate.

3. Add cinnamon and salt/pepper to taste.

4. Turn heat to low, add pine nuts.

5. Once filling is cool, add yogurt and mix. The yogurt prevents the filling from drying while baking.

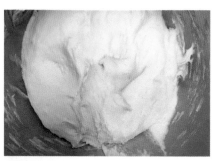

1 Dough is risen enough when it rebounds after pressing down with your finger gently.

2 Pinch off 1-inch diameter balls of dough.

3 Dipping each dough ball in the oil-butter mixture.

4 Flatten and spread balls out with fingers and let rest for 5 minutes.

5 Using your fingers spread each ball out until thin as tissue paper.

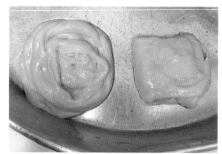

6 Either fold dough into a strip and roll into a rosette (left) or fold into a square (right).

7 Place folded dough into a baking pan coated with oil.

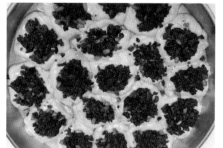

8 Place 1 1/2 teaspoon of filling on each dough base leaving a 1/2 inch edge clear.

Dough:

2 1/2 cups flour

1/2 teaspoon salt

1 cup warm water (40 degrees centigrade/100 degrees Fahrenheit)

1 teaspoon yeast

1/4 teaspoon sugar

1 1/2 tablespoons unsalted butter, melted

1 1/2 tablespoons vegetable oil

1. While filling cools, add yeast and sugar to 1/2 cup warm water to activate/rise.

2. Add flour, salt, yeast mix, and other 1/2 cup water to mixing bowl, and mix well.

3. Dough should be somewhat sticky but solid. Let proof for 30-45 minutes. Dough is risen enough when it rebounds after pressing down gently with your finger ❶.

4. In a microwavable bowl, add melted butter to oil. Warm slightly in microwave.

5. Dip fingers in oil-butter mixture, and pinch off 1-inch diameter balls of dough ❷,dipping each in the oil-butter mixture ❸. You should have about 20 balls.

6. Flatten and spread balls out with fingers and let rest for 5 minutes ❹.

7. After resting, coat fingers in oil to keep dough from sticking, and using your fingers spread each ball out until thin as tissue paper. If holes form in the dough, don't worry because folding is the next step ❺.

8. Folding: there are 2 techniques for folding

    a. Fold dough into a square 1x1 inch square (fold down, then fold ends across ❻, right)

    b. Fold dough into a strip and roll together (like a rosette ❻, left)

9. Place folded dough into a baking pan coated with oil. Press down so bottom of pan is covered in dough ❼.

Baking:

1. Place 1 1/2 teaspoon of filling on each dough base leaving a 1/2 inch edge clear ❽.

2. Preheat oven to 350 degrees Fahrenheit.

3. Bake for 30 minutes or until top of crust begins to brown, and the bottom is crisp and golden.

Eat with

Plain yogurt.

Desserts

صحّتين

Ghraybeh غريبه

Delicate Powdered Sugar Cookies

Active time: 30 minutes   **Baking/refrigeration time: 45 minutes**   Makes: 20-30

2 1/2 cups flour

1 1/4 cups lard or butter (Crisco OK)

3/4 cup powdered sugar

1/4 cup corn starch

1/2 teaspoon Arak (anise flavored distilled drink)

1. Beat the lard with an electric beater until fluffy, about 5 minutes. Add sugar and beat again. Add Arak and beat again to incorporate.

2. Sift flour and corn starch and add to sugar/lard mixture, in 1/2 cup increments, beating every time. The dough will come together.

3. Refrigerate dough for 30 minutes.

4. Remove from fridge and divide into small walnut-size balls.

5. Roll each ball into a log, 1/2 inch thick, 4 inches long. Bring ends of log together into a circle or pretzel shape and seal. You can decorate the seal with a pine nut.

6. Bake in 300 degree Fahrenheit oven, for 12 minutes, or until the bottoms are light golden brown, and tops look dry.

7. Remove from oven and let cool completely in pan on rack. Do not touch, very delicate and tend to break when warm.

Eat with

Turkish coffee or tea.

1 Spread the dough in a 9-inch round pan with sides.

2 Crumble or slice the cheese into thin slices and spread evenly on top of the dough in pan

3 Pour the hot pudding on top of the cheese in the pan

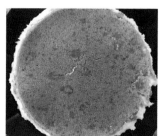

4 Invert onto a platter larger than the pan to make sure it doesn't overflow.

Knaffeh bil Jibin كنافه بالجبن
Sweet Semolina Crust with Sweet Cheese Filling

In Lebanon, this is a special breakfast you buy from the patisserie. The warm knafeh is stuffed in a sesame bun called ka'ak and drizzled with the sweet syrup called ater – irresistible.

Active time: 30 minutes   **Baking time: 40-50 minutes**   Serves 4

Traditionally, this is made with Arabic sweet white cheese. Fresh mozzarella is a good substitute.

Crust:

4 hot dog buns
4 tablespoon salted butter, room temperature
One 8 ounce ball fresh mozzarella cheese

1. Put the bread in the food processor and process until fine. Pour out the processed bread into a bowl and add the butter. Mix until dough is formed. Spread the dough in a 9-inch round pan with sides or pan with similar area ❶.

2. Crumble or slice the cheese into thin slices and spread evenly on top of the dough in pan ❷.

Pudding topping:

1/2 cup semolina (ground durum wheat)
4 cups whole milk
1 teaspoon of orange blossom water, rose blossom water, or both (optional)

3. Prepare the pudding. Put the milk in a saucepan, add the semolina, stir to mix and cook over medium heat until simmering, stirring the whole time to prevent sticking. When the pudding thickens (about 10-15 min), remove from heat. You can now add 1 teaspoon orange blossom water or rose water if you like. Pour the hot pudding on top of the cheese in the pan ❸.

4. Cover the pan with foil and bake in a preheated oven at 350 degrees Fahrenheit, on the center rack until the edges are bubbling and golden brown (about 1 hour).

5. Remove from the oven, cut around edges of knafeh to help release it from pan sides, and invert onto a platter larger than the pan to make sure it doesn't overflow ❹.

6. Slice & serve hot, passing ater separately.

Sugar syrup or Ater:

2 cups sugar
1 cup water
1 teaspoon fresh lemon juice
1 teaspoon orange water or rose water

In a saucepan, over medium heat, combine sugar and water and stir until dissolved. When completely dissolved and starting to boil, add the lemon juice. Continue boiling on low heat until thickened, about 5-7 minutes. When cool, you can add 1 teaspoon orange blossom water or rose water.

Extras

صحتين

Tarator طراطور

Lebanese Tartar Sauce

Active/total time: 10 minutes

  Makes about 1/2 cup

3 tablespoons lemon juice

3 tablespoons tahini

1 clove peeled garlic, crushed with 1 teapoon salt

Crush the garlic with salt until creamy. Add the lemon juice and mix well. Add tahini and mix until it is smooth and comes together. Done.

You can add 1 teaspoon of chopped parsley for a variation.

Note

Good with baked or fried seafood, kafta, falafel, as dip for veggies, spread on bread as a substitute for mayonnaise.

1 Place turnips in a jar.

2 Add beet slice, brine, and vinegar.

3 Ready in 48 hours.

صحتين

Lifit لفت

Pickled Turnips

Active time: 10 minutes   Pickling time: 48 hours   VG   Serves 4

1 pound turnips, medium size

1 cup boiled water

1 teaspoon salt

1 cup vinegar (white vinegar, apple cider vinegar, or rice vinegar), more or less

1 slice of a beet, raw or boiled, for color (optional)

1. Wash and peel turnips. Slice into 1/2 inch wide pieces, stick or half moon shape. Place in a clean mason jar, or jar with a well sealing cover ❶. Add beet slice if using (the beet will turn the turnips pink, and pinker the more beets you add).

2. To make brine, add salt to boiled water and stir to dissolve.

3. Add enough brine to cover halfway up the turnips. You may not need all of the brine, or may need more ❷.

4. Add vinegar to cover the turnips.

5. Seal jar and place on counter at room temperature. Should be ready in 48 hours ❸.

Index